1/07

Bravo!

WAHOO!

If you were an

Interjection

by Nancy Loewen
illustrated by Sara Gray

OOPS!

OH NO!

PICTURE WINDOW BOOKS
Minneapolis, Minnesota

interjection (interj) a word or phrase that shows strong feeling or emotion

Editor: Christianne Jones
Designer: Tracy Kaehler
Page Production: Lori Bye
Creative Director: Keith Griffin
Editorial Director: Carol Jones
The illustrations in this book were created with acrylics.

Picture Window Books
5115 Excelsior Boulevard
Suite 232
Minneapolis, MN 55416
877-845-8392
www.picturewindowbooks.com

Library of Congress Cataloging-in-Publication Data
Loewen, Nancy, 1964–
If you were an interjection / by Nancy Loewen ; illustrated by
Sara Gray.
p. cm. — (Word fun)
Includes bibliographical references.
ISBN-13: 978-1-4048-2636-6 (hardcover)
ISBN-10: 1-4048-2636-X (hardcover)
ISBN-13: 978-1-4048-2638-0 (paperback)
ISBN-10: 1-4048-2638-6 (paperback)
1. English language—Interjections—Juvenile literature. 1. Gray, Sara, ill.
II. Title. III. Series.
PE1355.L64 2006
425—dc22
2006003394

Special thanks to our advisers for their expertise:

Rosemary G. Palmer, Ph.D., Department of Literacy
College of Education, Boise State University

Susan Kesselring, M.A., Literacy Educator
Rosemount—Apple Valley—Eagan (Minnesota) School District

Looking for interjections?

Watch for the big, colorful words in the example sentences.

If you were an interjection, you would be a word or phrase that shows strong feeling or emotion.

SHOOT! I can't find my wallet.

OH! I found it. **SUPER!**

7

If you were an interjection, you would often be used with an exclamation point.

OOPS! I didn't mean to bump into you.

OH NO!
I spilled my milk.

YIKES!
What a mess!

If you were an interjection, you could also be used with a question mark or a comma.

WELL?

Are you coming?

HUH?

What did you say?

10

If you were an interjection, you would show feeling. You could show surprise and excitement. You could show disgust and fear.

HOORAY!

Here comes the parade.

WOW, do you see how much candy the clowns are throwing at the crowd?

YUCK! I'm glad I don't have to march behind that horse.

If you were an interjection, you could get a person's attention with a greeting or a farewell.

GOODBYE, Sammy!

GATE'S Guitar Lessons

HELLO, Mr. Gates.

If you were an interjection, you could be a filler word. You would give the speaker more time to get his or her thoughts together.

UH, where did you get those note cards?

WELL ... HELLO, I seem to have lost the note cards for my speech.

That's, **UM,** a good question—a very good question indeed.

If you were an interjection, you could be total nonsense and still add meaning to the sentence.

OOH-LA-LA, don't you look nice!

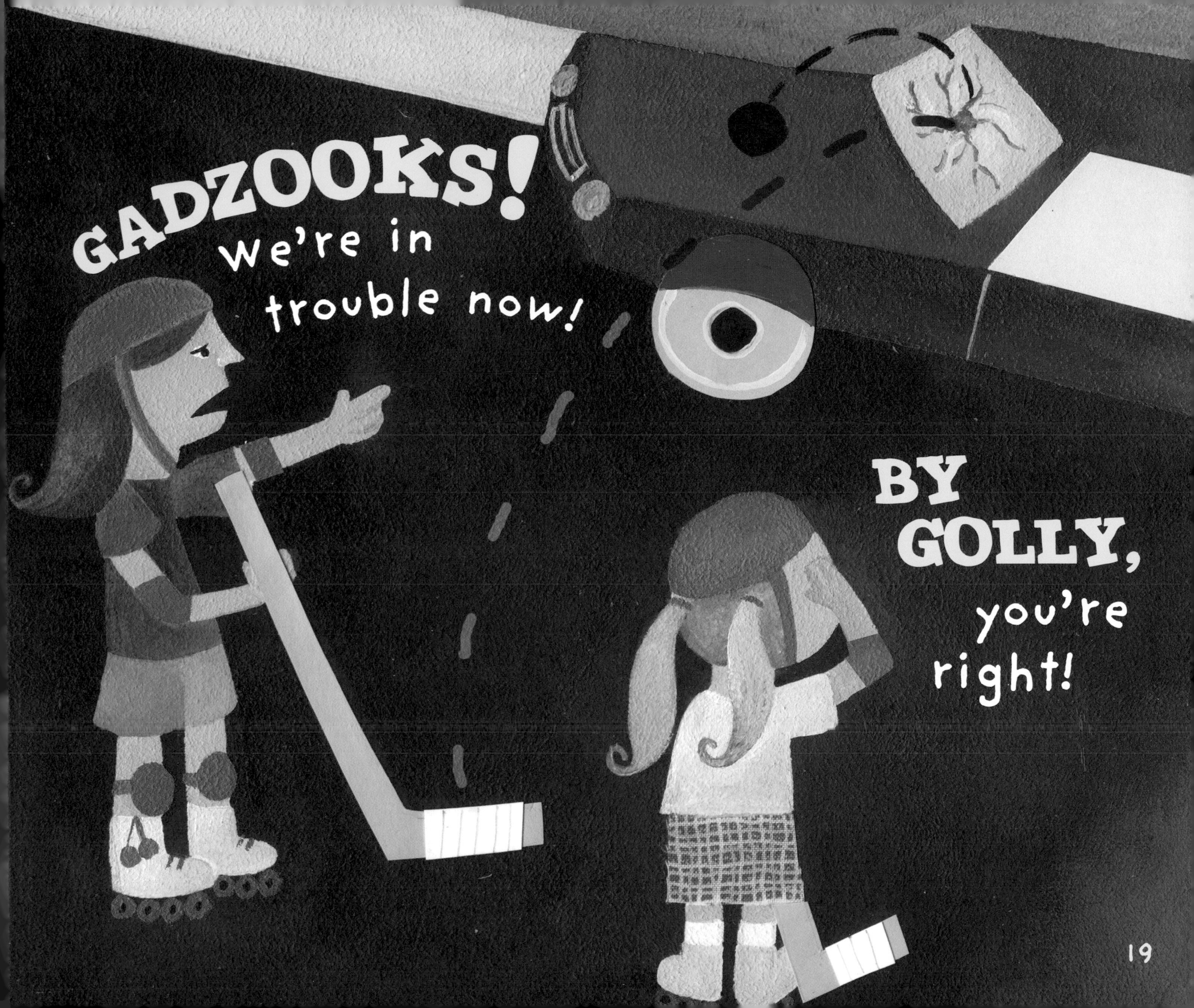
GADZOOKS! we're in trouble now!
BY GOLLY, you're right!

If you were an interjection, you could be a simple word used in many ways.

OH, I don't know if we can catch him.

OH? You really think we should try this?

OH! That's really gross!

Fun with Interjections

Interjections are often some of the funniest, most colorful words in our language. Take the word **PHEW**, for example. We use it when something doesn't smell good. Can you make up another interjection that might express the same feeling? How about **ACKMOO** or **HUFFKA**? Why not make up some of your own?

Make up interjections that could be used in the following situations:

1. When you see a big spider on the ceiling.

2. When you step on a melted ice-cream cone in the parking lot.

3. When your little sister grabs the last chocolate cupcake.

4. When your parents make leftover surprise for supper.

5. When you get into trouble for something you didn't do.

Get together with your friends and hold a contest. Have one person judge the best new interjections. Then you can all start using the winning words.

Fact: If you look up an interjection in the dictionary, you will see the abbreviation "interj" next to it. The "interj" stands for interjection.

Glossary

address—to speak to another person

emotion—a strong feeling

interjection—a word or phrase that shows strong feeling or emotion

nonsense—acting or speaking in a silly way or in a way that doesn't make sense

phrase—a group of words that expresses a thought but is not a complete sentence

To Learn More

At the Library

Heinrichs, Ann. *Interjections.* Chanhassen, Minn.: Child's World, 2004.

Heller, Ruth. *Fantastic! Wow! And Unreal! A Book about Interjections and Conjunctions.* New York: Grosset & Dunlap, 1998.

On the Web

FactHound offers a safe, fun way to find Internet sites related to this book. All of the sites on FactHound have been researched by our staff.

1. Visit *www.facthound.com*
2. Type in this special code for age-appropriate sites: 140482636X
3. Click on the FETCH IT button.

Your trusty FactHound will fetch the best sites for you!

Index

Look for all of the books in the Word Fun series: